Family of Faith Library

HELPING CHILDREN LEARN MATHEMATICS

W9-BEC-235

Mathematics Learning Study Committee

Jeremy Kilpatrick and Jane Swafford, Editors

Center for Education
Division of Behavioral and Social Sciences and Education
National Research Council

Property of
FAMILY OF FAITH
LIBRARY

NATIONAL ACADEMY PRESS
WASHINGTON, DC

NATIONAL ACADEMY PRESS • 2101 Constitution Avenue, NW • Washington, DC 20418

NOTICE: The project that is the subject of this report was approved by the Governing Board of the National Research Council, whose members are drawn from the councils of the National Academy of Sciences, the National Academy of Engineering, and the Institute of Medicine. The members of the committee responsible for the report were chosen for their special competences and with regard for appropriate balance.

This study was supported by Contract/Grant No. ESI-9816818 between the National Academy of Sciences and the ExxonMobil Foundation. Additional support was also provided by the U.S. Department of Education and the National Science Foundation. Any opinions, findings, conclusions, or recommendations expressed in this publication are those of the authors and do not necessarily reflect the views of the organizations or agencies that provided support for the project.

International Standard Book Number 0-309-08431-8
Library of Congress Catalog Control Number: 2002106187

Additional copies of this report are available from National Academy Press, 2101 Constitution Avenue, NW, Lockbox 285, Washington, DC 20055; (800) 624-6242 or (202) 334-3313 (in the Washington metropolitan area); Internet, http://www.nap.edu

Printed in the United States of America
Copyright 2002 by the National Academy of Sciences. All rights reserved.

Suggested citation: National Research Council. (2002). *Helping Children Learn Mathematics.* Mathematics Learning Study Committee, J. Kilpatrick and J. Swafford, Editors. Center for Education, Division of Behavioral and Social Sciences and Education. Washington, DC: National Academy Press.

First Printing, August 2002
Second Printing, November 2002

THE NATIONAL ACADEMIES

Advisers to the Nation on Science, Engineering, and Medicine

The **National Academy of Sciences** is a private, nonprofit, self-perpetuating society of distinguished scholars engaged in scientific and engineering research, dedicated to the furtherance of science and technology and to their use for the general welfare. Upon the authority of the charter granted to it by the Congress in 1863, the Academy has a mandate that requires it to advise the federal government on scientific and technical matters. Dr. Bruce M. Alberts is president of the National Academy of Sciences.

The **National Academy of Engineering** was established in 1964, under the charter of the National Academy of Sciences, as a parallel organization of outstanding engineers. It is autonomous in its administration and in the selection of its members, sharing with the National Academy of Sciences the responsibility for advising the federal government. The National Academy of Engineering also sponsors engineering programs aimed at meeting national needs, encourages education and research, and recognizes the superior achievements of engineers. Dr. Wm. A. Wulf is president of the National Academy of Engineering.

The **Institute of Medicine** was established in 1970 by the National Academy of Sciences to secure the services of eminent members of appropriate professions in the examination of policy matters pertaining to the health of the public. The Institute acts under the responsibility given to the National Academy of Sciences by its congressional charter to be an adviser to the federal government and, upon its own initiative, to identify issues of medical care, research, and education. Dr. Harvey V. Fineberg is president of the Institute of Medicine.

The **National Research Council** was organized by the National Academy of Sciences in 1916 to associate the broad community of science and technology with the Academy's purposes of furthering knowledge and advising the federal government. Functioning in accordance with general policies determined by the Academy, the Council has become the principal operating agency of both the National Academy of Sciences and the National Academy of Engineering in providing services to the government, the public, and the scientific and engineering communities. The Council is administered jointly by both Academies and the Institute of Medicine. Dr. Bruce M. Alberts and Dr. Wm. A. Wulf are chairman and vice chairman, respectively, of the National Research Council.

MATHEMATICS LEARNING STUDY COMMITTEE

JEREMY KILPATRICK, *Chair,* University of Georgia
DEBORAH LOEWENBERG BALL, University of Michigan
HYMAN BASS, University of Michigan
JERE BROPHY, Michigan State University
FELIX BROWDER, Rutgers University
THOMAS P. CARPENTER, University of Wisconsin-Madison
CAROLYN DAY, Dayton Public Schools
KAREN FUSON, Northwestern University
JAMES HIEBERT, University of Delaware
ROGER HOWE, Yale University
CAROLYN KIERAN, University of Quebec, Montreal
RICHARD E. MAYER, University of California, Santa Barbara
KEVIN MILLER, University of Illinois, Urbana-Champaign
CASILDA PARDO, Albuquerque Public Schools
EDGAR ROBINSON, ExxonMobil Corporation (Retired)
HUNG HSI WU, University of California, Berkeley

JANE SWAFFORD, *Study Director*
BRADFORD FINDELL, *Program Officer*
BRIAN McQUILLAN, *Senior Project Assistant*
CAROLE LACAMPAGNE, *Director,* Mathematical Sciences Education Board

Acknowledgments

In preparing this book, we had the good fortune of working with a number of people who shared our enthusiasm for the project, and we are indebted to them for the insights and assistance they provided. The entire Mathematics Learning Study Committee contributed valuable ideas, but we particularly acknowledge the members of the subcommittee who conceptualized and shaped the book: Thomas Carpenter, James Hiebert, Casilda Pardo, and Edgar Robinson. We are grateful to them for their inspiration, hard work, and guidance. During the outlining and preliminary drafting of the book, we benefited from the views and prose provided by Pat McNees, a writer consultant. And we are especially indebted to Steve Olson, who took our rough drafts and sketchy ideas and turned them into this final product. Without his expert editorial assistance, the project might never have been completed.

We would like to thank our sponsor for this book, the ExxonMobil Foundation, for seeking to engage a much broader audience in discussion and action. In particular, we thank Edward Ahnert, president of the Foundation, and Joe Gonzales, program officer, for their support and interest. We also want to thank the sponsors of the Mathematics Learning Study, the National Science Foundation and the U.S. Department of Education, for their continued support during the production of the book.

This book has been reviewed by individuals chosen for their diverse perspectives and technical expertise, in accordance with procedures approved by the National Research Council's (NRC) Report Review Committee. The purpose of this independent review is to provide candid and critical comments that will assist the institution in making its published book as sound as possible and to ensure that the book meets institutional standards for objectivity, evidence, and responsiveness to the study charge. The review comments and draft manuscript remain confidential to protect the integrity of the deliberative process. We thank the following individuals for their review of this book: Arthur J. Baroody, Department of Curriculum and Instruction, University of Illinois; Keith Devlin, Center for the Study of Language and Information, Stanford University; Nancy A. Doorey, Brandywine School District, Delaware; Andrew M. Gleason, Department of Mathematics, Harvard University; Nancy Larson, West Haven Schools, Connecticut; Mike Riley, Bellevue School District, Washington; Zalman P. Usiskin, Department of Education, University of Chicago; and Carrie L. Valentine, Madison Metropolitan School District and University of Wisconsin.

Although the reviewers listed above have provided many constructive comments and suggestions, they were not asked to endorse the conclusions or recommendations, nor did they see the final draft of the book before its release. The review of this book was overseen by Alfred Manaster, University of California at San Diego, and Patrick Suppes, Stanford University. Appointed by the NRC, they were responsible for making certain that an independent examination of this book was carried out in accordance with institutional procedures and that all review comments were carefully considered. Responsibility for the final content of this book rests solely with the authoring committee and the NRC.

Finally, we extend our sincere thanks to a number of individuals at the NRC who made significant contributions to our work: Michael J. Feuer, director of the Center for Education (CFE), for providing key advice; Kirsten Sampson Snyder, reports officer for CFE, for guiding us through the report review process; Bradford Findell, former program officer, for his contributions to several drafts; Patricia Morison, senior program officer, for shepherding this project through its final stages; Sally Stanfield and Francesca Moghari, National Academy Press, for making our book look so nice; Carole Lacampagne for her wise advice during late stages; and Dionna Williams and Yvonne Wise for help with production. Last, we would like to express our appreciation to Brian McQuillan, senior project assistant, who provided a wealth of logistical support during the project.

Jeremy Kilpatrick, *Chair*
Jane Swafford, *Study Director*
Mathematics Learning Study Committee

Contents

Overview

The major observations and recommendations of this book establish new goals for mathematics learning and lay out a course of action for achieving those goals.

- All students can and should be proficient in mathematics.
- Mathematical proficiency involves five intertwined strands: (1) understanding mathematics; (2) computing fluently; (3) applying concepts to solve problems; (4) reasoning logically; and (5) engaging with mathematics, seeing it as sensible, useful, and doable.
- For all students to become mathematically proficient, major changes must be made in mathematics instruction, instructional materials, assessments, teacher education, and the broader educational system. In particular:
  —Instruction should support the development of mathematical proficiency for all.
  —Instructional materials should integrate the five strands of mathematical proficiency.
  —Assessments should contribute to the goal of mathematical proficiency.
  —Teachers should have the support that will enable them to teach all students to be mathematically proficient.
  —Efforts to achieve mathematical proficiency for all students must be coordinated, comprehensive, and informed by scientific evidence.
- Mathematical proficiency for all cannot be achieved through piecemeal or isolated efforts. All interested parties—including parents and caregivers, teachers, administrators, and policy makers—must work together to improve school mathematics.

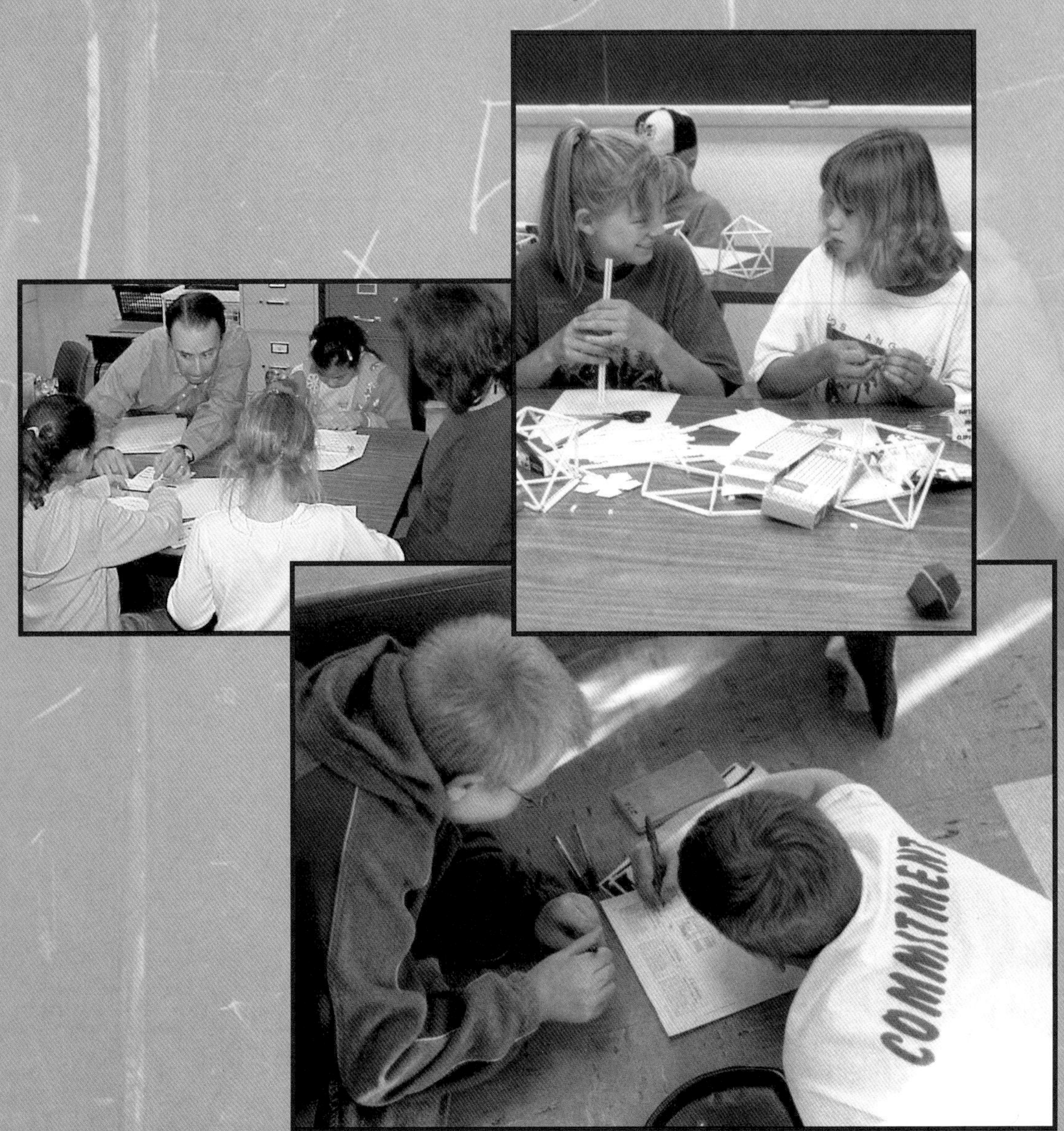
COMMITMENT

Introduction

Today the United States has the challenge and the opportunity to provide all students with the mathematical knowledge, skills, and confidence they will need in a highly technical world. There is considerable nationwide interest in improving students' understanding of mathematics, combined with an emerging consensus about the essential elements of mathematics instruction; in addition, research has provided valuable insights into how children learn. Together these factors are opening the way to substantial and enduring progress in school mathematics.

Greater understanding of mathematics will be essential for today's schoolchildren. Success in tomorrow's job market will require more than computational competence. It will require the ability to apply mathematical knowledge to solve problems. If today's students are to compete successfully in the world of tomorrow, they must be able to learn new concepts and skills. They need to view mathematics as a tool they can use every day. They need to have the mathematical sophistication that will enable them to take full advantage of the information and communication technologies that permeate our homes and workplaces. Students with a poor understanding of mathematics will have fewer opportunities to pursue higher levels of education and to compete for good jobs.

Despite the dramatically increased role of mathematics in our society, mathematics classrooms in the United States today too often resemble their counterparts of a century ago.[1] Many mathematics teachers still spend the bulk of their class time demonstrating procedures and supervising students while they practice those procedures. In numerous elementary and middle schools, time for learning mathematics is too brief. Textbooks are typically packed with an assortment of topics, so that the treatment of any one topic is often both shallow and repetitive. Key ideas can be difficult to pick out from among the many incidental details. This scattered and superficial curriculum means that students learn much less than they might. They then take standardized tests that often measure low-level skills rather than the kind of problem-solving abilities needed in modern life. All too often, mathematics instruction serves to alienate students rather than to reveal to them the beauty and usefulness of mathematics.

Despite its remarkable stability, school mathematics has changed somewhat in the United States over the past decade or so. Some districts are using instructional materials that are more likely to lead to mathematical proficiency, and some states have developed tests to measure more than low-level skills. More teachers are effectively engaging students with worthwhile mathematics. However, progress has been uneven and poorly documented.

Results from national and international assessments indicate that schoolchildren in the United States are not learning mathematics well enough. During the 1990s, performance on national assessments did improve in some areas of mathematics and for some groups of students. For example, fourth and eighth graders made significant gains. Performance also improved among black and Hispanic students, although the gap between the performance of these students and that of white students remains large. Even with these gains, however, performance is still below what is needed of U.S. students.[2] Many students cannot use computations to solve problems. Their understanding and use of decimals and fractions are especially weak. In international comparisons, their mathematics performance is usually no better than average and sometimes below that.

Helping all children succeed in mathematics is an imperative national goal. Yet, although there is ample research on the learning of mathematics, there is a shortage of comprehensive and reliable information gleaned from that research to guide efforts to improve school mathematics.

Frequently Asked Questions

Shaded boxes appearing throughout this book address the following questions, which arise in discussions of school mathematics:

This short book is based on *Adding It Up: Helping Children Learn Mathematics.* Both are products of the National Research Council's Mathematics Learning Study Committee, a multidisciplinary group of scholars, educators, researchers, and administrators with differing perspectives on school mathematics but a shared commitment to making it as effective as possible. Our committee has sought to move the discussion beyond the narrow views that have characterized past debates about how to improve student learning. We have not focused on a particular aspect of school mathematics, such as the curriculum or textbooks. Instead, we have taken a comprehensive view of what it means to be successful in mathematics. By examining, debating, and synthesizing the available research evidence, we have come to a consensus about how school mathematics needs to change to prepare students for life in the 21st century.

This book examines school mathematics during a critical period in a child's education—from pre-kindergarten (pre-K) through eighth grade. During these years, students need to become proficient in mathematics if they are to be successful at higher levels of education and in the workplace. This book focuses on the domain of *number,* which is at the heart of preschool, elementary school, and middle school mathematics. Many of the controversies about school mathematics concern the learning of number, and it is the most thoroughly investigated part of the curriculum. But our concentration on number is not meant to imply that school mathematics from pre-K through eighth grade should be limited to arithmetic. On the contrary, school mathematics in the early grades needs to give significant attention to additional mathematical domains, such as algebra, geometry, probability, and statistics. We use the domain of number to illustrate what might be done throughout the curriculum.

This book, *Helping Children Learn Mathematics,* is addressed to parents and caregivers, teachers, administrators, and policy makers, all of whom must work together to improve mathematics learning. The book concludes with lists of recommended actions for each of these groups. Many other groups also must contribute, including textbook publishers, the creators of state and national learning standards and assessments, and education researchers. For those groups, *Adding It Up* provides more detailed guidance.

The Origins of This Book

In 1998 the National Science Foundation and the U.S. Department of Education asked the National Research Council to conduct a study of what research says about successful mathematics learning from the preschool years through eighth grade. The National Research Council, which is the principal operating agency of the National Academy of Sciences, established a committee of 16 people to carry out this task. The charge to the committee had three parts:

1. to synthesize the rich and diverse research on pre-kindergarten through eighth-grade mathematics learning;
2. to provide research-based recommendations for teaching, teacher education, and curriculum for improving student learning and to identify areas where research is needed;
3. to give advice and guidance to educators, researchers, publishers, policy makers, and parents.

The Mathematics Learning Study Committee included school practitioners, research mathematicians, educational researchers, and a retired business executive. Committee members differed not only in expertise but in viewpoint—at the beginning of the committee's work its members had many different and contrasting ideas about how mathematics learning can and should be improved. Over the course of eighteen months and eight meetings, the committee reviewed and synthesized the relevant research, gathered materials from commissioned papers and presentations, and discussed mathematics learning in light of the many and varied experiences of its members. In the process, the committee members gradually arrived at a consensus about the changes needed in mathematics teaching, teacher education, and the mathematics curriculum.

The committee's final book benefited from the efforts of many different people concerned with improving mathematics education. The book *Adding It Up: Helping Children Learn Mathematics* can be purchased from the National Academy Press at 800-624-6242; it is also available on the World Wide Web at http://www.nap.edu/catalog/9822.html.

To disseminate the major conclusions of *Adding It Up* to a broader audience, a subcommittee of the Mathematics Learning Study Committee has overseen the production of this short book.

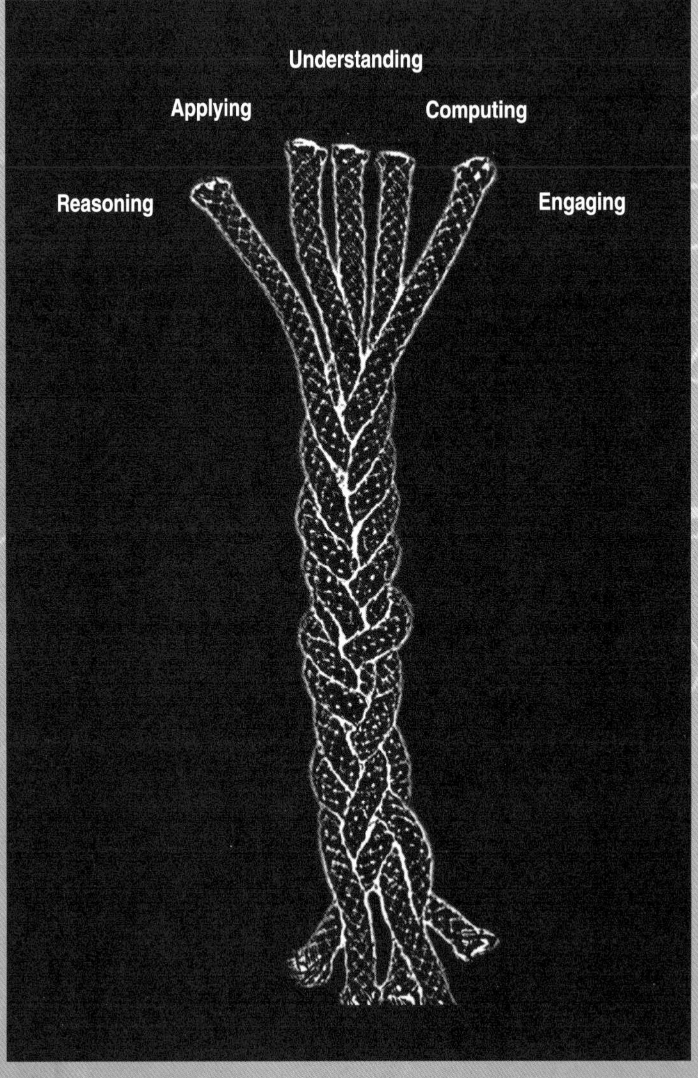
Understanding
Applying
Computing
Reasoning
Engaging

What Does It Mean to Be Successful in Mathematics?

Our analyses of the mathematics to be learned, our reading of the research in cognitive psychology and mathematics education, our experience as learners and teachers of mathematics, and our professional judgment have led us to adopt a composite view of successful mathematics learning. Recognizing that no term completely captures all aspects of expertise, competence, knowledge, and facility in mathematics, we have chosen *mathematical proficiency* to express what we think it means for anyone to learn mathematics successfully.

Mathematical proficiency has five strands:[3]

(1) Understanding: Comprehending mathematical concepts, operations, and relations—knowing what mathematical symbols, diagrams, and procedures mean.

(2) Computing: Carrying out mathematical procedures, such as adding, subtracting, multiplying, and dividing numbers flexibly, accurately, efficiently, and appropriately.

(3) Applying: Being able to formulate problems mathematically and to devise strategies for solving them using concepts and procedures appropriately.

(4) Reasoning: Using logic to explain and justify a solution to a problem or to extend from something known to something not yet known.

(5) Engaging: Seeing mathematics as sensible, useful, and doable—*if* you work at it—and being willing to do the work.

The most important feature of mathematical proficiency is that these five strands are interwoven and interdependent. Other views of mathematics learning have tended to emphasize only one aspect of proficiency, with the expectation that other aspects will develop as a consequence. For example, some people who have emphasized the need for students to master computations have assumed that understanding would follow. Others, focusing on students' understanding of concepts, have assumed that skill would develop naturally. By using these five strands, we have attempted to give a more rounded portrayal of successful mathematics learning.

The overriding premise of this book is that all students can and should achieve mathematical proficiency. Just as all students can become proficient readers, all can become proficient in school mathematics. Mathematical proficiency is not something students accomplish only when they reach eighth or twelfth grade; they can be proficient regardless of their grade. Moreover, mathematical proficiency can no longer be restricted to a select few. All young Americans must learn to think mathematically if the United States is to foster the educated workforce and citizenry tomorrow's world will demand.

The Five Strands

(1) Understanding: Comprehending mathematical concepts, operations, and relations—knowing what mathematical symbols, diagrams, and procedures mean.

Understanding refers to a student's grasp of fundamental mathematical ideas. Students with understanding know more than isolated facts and procedures. They know why a mathematical idea is important and the contexts in which it is useful. Furthermore, they are aware of many connections between mathematical ideas. In fact, the degree of students' understanding is related to the richness and extent of the connections they have made.

For example, students who understand division of fractions not only can compute $6 \div \frac{2}{3} = 9$. They also can represent the operation by a diagram and make up a problem to go with the computation. (If a recipe calls for $\frac{2}{3}$ cup of sugar and 6 cups of sugar are available, how many batches of the recipe can be made with the available sugar?)

Students who learn with understanding have less to learn because they see common patterns in superficially different situations. If they understand the general principle that the order in which two numbers are multiplied doesn't matter—3×5 is the same as 5×3, for example—they have about half as many "number facts" to learn. Or if students understand the general principle that multiplying the dimensions of a three-dimensional object by a factor n increases its volume by the factor n^3, they can understand many situations in which objects of all shapes are proportionally expanded or shrunk. (They can understand, for example, why a 16-ounce cup that has the same shape as an 8-ounce cup is much less than twice as tall.)

Knowledge learned with understanding provides a foundation for remembering or reconstructing mathematical facts and methods, for solving new and unfamiliar problems, and for generating new knowledge. For example, students who thoroughly understand whole number operations can extend these concepts and procedures to operations involving decimals.

Understanding also helps students to avoid critical errors in problem solving—especially problems of magnitude. Any student with good number sense who multiplies 9.83 and 7.65 and gets 7,519.95 for an answer should immediately see that something is wrong. The answer can't be more than 10 times 8 or 80, as one number is less than 10 and the other is less than 8. This reasoning should suggest to the student that the decimal point has been misplaced.

(2) Computing: Carrying out mathematical procedures, such as adding, subtracting, multiplying, and dividing numbers flexibly, accurately, efficiently, and appropriately.

Computing includes being fluent with procedures for adding, subtracting, multiplying, and dividing mentally or with paper and pencil, and knowing when and how to use these procedures appropriately. Although the word *computing* implies an arithmetic procedure, in this document it also refers to being fluent with procedures from other branches of mathematics, such as measurement (measuring lengths), algebra (solving equations), geometry (constructing similar figures), and statistics (graphing data). *Being fluent* means having the skill to perform the procedure efficiently, accurately, and flexibly.

Students need to compute basic number combinations ($6 + 7$, $17 - 9$, 8×4, and so on) rapidly and accurately. They also need to become accurate and efficient with algorithms—step-by-step procedures for adding, subtracting, multiplying, and dividing multi-digit whole numbers, fractions, and decimals, and for doing other computations. For example, all students should have an algorithm for multiplying 64 and 37 that they understand, that is reasonably efficient and general enough to be used with other two-digit numbers, and that can be extended to use with larger numbers.

The use of calculators need not threaten the development of students' computational skills. On the contrary, calculators can enhance both understanding

Which side of the "math wars" is correct?

Reform efforts during the 1980s and 1990s downplayed computational skill, emphasizing instead that students should understand and be able to use math. In extreme cases, students were expected to invent math with little or no assistance. Reactions to these efforts led to increased attention to memorization and computational skill, with students expected to internalize procedures presented by teachers or textbooks. The clash of these contrasting positions has been called the "math wars."

Which position is correct? Neither. Both are too narrow. When people advocate only one strand of proficiency, they lose sight of the overall goal. Such a narrow treatment of math may well be one reason for the poor performance of U.S. students in national and international assessments.

Math instruction cannot be effective if it is based on extreme positions. Students become more proficient when they understand the underlying concepts of math, and they understand the concepts more easily if they are skilled at computational procedures. U.S. students need more skill and more understanding along with the ability to apply concepts to solve problems, to reason logically, and to see math as sensible, useful, and doable. Anything less leads to knowledge that is fragile, disconnected, and weak.

and computing.[4] But as with any instructional tool, calculators and computers can be used effectively or not so effectively. Teachers need to learn how to use these tools—and teach students to use them—in ways that support and integrate the strands of proficiency.

Accuracy and efficiency with procedures are important, but computing also supports understanding. By working through procedures that are general enough for solving a whole class of problems, such as a procedure for adding any two fractions, students gain appreciation for the fact that mathematics is predictable, well structured, and filled with patterns.

When students merely memorize procedures, they may fail to understand the deeper ideas that could make it easier to remember—and apply—what they learn. When they are subtracting, for example, many children subtract the smaller number from the larger in each column, no matter where it is, so wrong answers like the following are common:

$$\begin{array}{r} 62 \\ \underline{-\ 48} \\ 26 \end{array} \qquad \text{(instead of 14)}$$

Children who learn to subtract with understanding rarely make this kind of error.[5]

Developing computational skill and developing understanding are often seen as competing for attention in school mathematics. But pitting skill against understanding creates a false dichotomy. Understanding makes it easier to learn skills, while learning procedures can strengthen and develop mathematical understanding.

(3) Applying: Being able to formulate problems mathematically and to devise strategies for solving them using concepts and procedures appropriately.

Applying involves using one's conceptual and procedural knowledge to solve problems. A concept or procedure is not useful unless students recognize when and where to use it—as well as when and where it does not apply. In school, students are given specific problems to solve, but outside school they encounter situations in which part of the difficulty is figuring out exactly what the problem is. Therefore, students also need to be able to pose problems, devise solution strategies, and choose the most useful strategy for solving problems. They need to know how to picture quantities in their minds or draw them on paper, and they need to know how to distinguish what is known and relevant from what is unknown.

Routine problems can always be solved using standard procedures. For example, most children in second grade know that they must add to answer the following question: "If 12 students are on the minibus and 7 more get on, how many students are on the bus?" But for nonroutine problems, students must invent a way to understand and solve the problem. For example, second graders might be asked the following question: "A minibus has 7 seats that hold 2 or 3 students each. If there are 19 students, how many must sit 2 to a seat, and how many must sit 3 to a seat?" To come up with an answer, they must invent a solution method. They need to understand the quantities in the problem and their relationships, and they must have the computing skills required to solve the problem.

(4) Reasoning: Using logic to explain and justify a solution to a problem or to extend from something known to something not yet known.

Reasoning is the glue that holds mathematics together. By thinking about the logical relationships between concepts and situations, students can navigate through the elements of a problem and see how they fit together. If provided with opportunities to explore and discuss even and odd numbers, for example, fourth graders can explain why the sum of any even and any odd number will be odd.

One of the best ways for students to improve their reasoning is to explain or justify their solutions to others. Once a procedure for adding fractions has been developed, for example, students should sometimes be asked to explain and justify that procedure rather than just doing practice problems. In the process of communicating their thinking, they hone their reasoning skills.

Reasoning interacts strongly with the other strands of mathematical proficiency, especially when students are solving problems. As students reason about a problem, they can build their understanding, carry out the needed computations, apply their knowledge, explain their reasoning to others, and come to see mathematics as sensible and doable.

(5) Engaging: Seeing mathematics as sensible, useful, and doable—*if* you work at it—and being willing to do the work.

Engaging in mathematical activity is the key to success. Our view of mathematical proficiency goes beyond being able to understand, compute, apply, and

Do students still need to learn how to compute with paper and pencil now that calculators and computers are available?

Yes. The widespread availability of calculators has greatly reduced the need for performing complex calculations with paper and pencil. But students need to understand what is happening in these complex calculations, and they still need to learn to perform simpler computations with pencil and paper because that helps them develop math proficiency. For example, a certain level of skill with basic number combinations is needed to understand procedures for multiplying two-digit numbers, and computational fluency is often essential in solving problems in algebra and explaining their solutions. How much instructional time should be spent on complex pencil-and-paper calculations is a question that will need to be continually revisited over the next decades.

reason. It includes engagement with mathematics: Students should have a personal commitment to the idea that mathematics makes sense and that—given reasonable effort—they can learn it and use it, both in school and outside school. Students who are proficient in mathematics see it as sensible, useful, and worthwhile, and they believe that their efforts in learning it pay off; they see themselves as effective learners, doers, and users of mathematics.

Success in mathematics learning requires being positively disposed toward the subject. Students who are engaged with mathematics do not believe that there is some mysterious "math gene" that dictates success. They believe that with sufficient effort and experience they can learn. If students are to learn, do, and use mathematics effectively, they should not look at it as an arbitrary set of rules and procedures. They need to see it instead as a subject in which things fit together logically and sensibly, and they need to believe that they are capable of figuring it out.

Engaging oneself with mathematics requires frequent opportunities to make sense of it, to experience the rewards of making sense of it, and to recognize the benefits of perseverance. As students build their mathematical proficiency, they become more confident of their ability to learn mathematics and to use it. The more mathematical concepts they understand, the more sensible the whole subject becomes. In contrast, when they think mathematics needs to be learned by memorizing rather than by making sense of it, they begin to lose confidence in themselves as learners. Students who are proficient in mathematics believe that they can solve problems, develop understanding, and learn procedures through hard work, and that becoming mathematically proficient is worthwhile for them.

Integrating the Strands of Proficiency

Just as a stool cannot stand on one leg or even two, so mathematical proficiency cannot stand on one or two isolated strands. To become mathematically proficient, students need to develop all five strands throughout their elementary school and middle school years.

At any given moment during a mathematics lesson or unit, one or two strands might be emphasized. But all the strands must eventually be addressed so that the links among them are strengthened. For example, a lesson that has the main goal of developing students' understanding of a mathematical concept might also rely on problem solving and require a number of computations. Or students might be asked to reason about a newly introduced idea rather than simply being presented with a definition and examples. In addition, throughout the school year, students should have opportunities to focus on various strands in various combinations. If teachers routinely stress just one or two strands, ignoring the others, the mathematics their students learn is likely to be incomplete and fragile.

Developing the strands of proficiency individually is much harder than learning them together. In fact, it is almost impossible to master any one of the strands in isolation. This might be why it is so hard for students to remember, for example, all the rules for computing with fractions and decimals if that is all they learn. Addressing all the strands of proficiency makes knowledge stronger, more durable, more adaptable, more useful, and more relevant.

Integrating the strands of mathematical proficiency is entirely consistent with students' typical approaches to learning. For example, as a child gains understanding, he or she remembers computational procedures better and uses them more flexibly to solve problems. In turn, as a procedure becomes more automatic, the child can think of other aspects of a problem and can tackle new problems, which leads to new understanding. The box on page 18 provides a further description of the integration of the strands of mathematical proficiency.

U.S. school mathematics today often assumes that children must master certain skills before they can understand the procedures and apply them—as if children cannot play a tune before they have mastered all the scales. But students can figure out that there are five and a half $\frac{1}{2}$-foot lengths of ribbon in a $2\frac{3}{4}$-foot strip before they are taught to "invert and multiply." In fact, solving such problems can help students understand the invert-and-multiply procedure. They might, for example, observe that the number of $\frac{1}{2}$-foot lengths in 1 foot is two. Hence multiplying $2\frac{3}{4} \times 2$ (the reciprocal of $\frac{1}{2}$) will give the total number of $\frac{1}{2}$-foot lengths in the $2\frac{3}{4}$-foot strip.

Just as a symphony cannot be heard by listening to each instrument's part in succession, mathematical proficiency cannot be attained by learning each of the strands of proficiency in isolation. Instruction needs to take advantage of children's natural inclination to use all five strands of mathematical proficiency. (The box on pages 19-20 gives examples of how the strands of proficiency can be integrated in learning how to solve proportions.) In this way, students understand and know how to apply procedures that they are often expected merely to memorize.

Integrating the Strands of Proficiency in Learning Number Combinations

Learning to add, subtract, multiply, and divide with single-digit numbers has long been characterized in the United States as "learning basic facts or number combinations," and students traditionally have been expected simply to memorize those combinations. Research has shown, however, that students actually move through a fairly well-defined sequence of solution methods when they are learning to perform operations with single-digit numbers. This deeper understanding of student learning demonstrates how the four other strands of proficiency—in addition to computing—can be strengthened through the learning of number combinations.[6]

Understanding

Number combinations are related. Recognizing and taking advantage of these connections can make the learning of number combinations easier and less susceptible to forgetting and error. For example, students quickly learn that 5 cookies plus 4 cookies is one more than 4 cookies plus 4 cookies.

Students also learn some number combinations earlier than others. For example, they often learn doubles (e.g., $6 + 6$, $9 + 9$) and sums to ten (e.g., $7 + 3$) earlier than other number combinations, and they can use this knowledge to learn other number combinations (e.g., $6 + 7$ is one more than $6 + 6$; $8 + 5$ can be broken down into $8 + 2 + 3$).

Connections between addition and subtraction and between multiplication and division can be exploited to make it easier for students to learn subtraction and division number combinations. For example, $13 - 8$ can be thought of as the number that needs to be added to 8 to get 13. It is easier for many students to do subtraction in this building-up way, which is related to their knowledge of addition.

Applying

Learning number combinations can be treated as a problem-solving activity. Students use number combinations they know to generate number combinations they do not know. For example, because multiples of 5 are relatively easy to learn, a student can use his or her knowledge of 5×8 to find 6×8. It is $(5 \times 8) + 8$.

Reasoning

As students talk about how they figured out a particular number combination, they have an opportunity to explain how they did it. By explaining their solutions, they demonstrate and refine their understanding of the relevant relationships. An example might be: "I know that 4×6 is 24 because I know my fours. And 8×6 will be another four groups of six. So 8×6 is 24 plus 24, and that's 48."

Engaging

When they consider the relationships among number combinations, students see the learning of number combinations as sensible, not simply as the learning of arbitrary associations between numbers. They begin to see themselves as capable of using numbers to solve practical problems.

They also learn that they can generate number combinations if they forget them. They have resources to learn on their own and do not have to depend on a teacher to tell them whether they have the right answer.

Mathematical Proficiency in the Development of Proportional Reasoning

Results from national assessments indicate that solving proportion problems such as "If a girl can read 3 pages in 4 minutes, at this rate how many pages will she have read in 10 minutes?" is often difficult for U.S. eighth graders. However, when students are encouraged to explore proportional situations in a variety of problem contexts, they naturally draw on all the strands of mathematical proficiency. Further, encouraging them to integrate the strands while they are learning how to solve proportions can lead to higher achievement.[7] For an illustration of how students integrate the strands of proficiency, consider the work of several fifth-grade students who were given the following problem:[8]

Ellen, Jim, and Steve bought three helium-filled balloons priced at 3 for $2. They decided to go back to the store and buy enough balloons for everyone in the class. How much would they pay for 24 more balloons?

Belinda got the correct answer ($16) by drawing 24 circles on her paper and then crossing out three and writing $2. She continued to cross out circles in groups of three, keeping track of the $2 amounts in a column, and then added the column of $2s.

Damon divided 24 by 3 to arrive at $8; then he divided 24 by 2 to arrive at $12. Unable to reconcile his two answers, he resorted to using a set of cubes; he formed eight groups of three cubes each. He announced that the answer was \$16, explaining that because each pack of three balloons cost \$2 and there were eight packs, $2 \times 8 = 16$.

Marti calculated the unit price for one balloon by dividing \$2 by 3 on her calculator. She got 0.6667, which she called "a wacky number." She multiplied this result by 24 to get 16. Later, Marti was telling her older brother about the different ways the children in her class had solved the balloon problem. Her brother showed her another way by using equivalent fractions: \$2 for three balloons is equivalent to how much for 24 balloons? (That is, $\frac{\$2}{3} = \frac{?}{24}$.) He explained that because you multiply 3 by 8 to get 24, you must multiply 2 by 8 to get the missing numerator. So the answer is \$16.

The ways in which these children solved the problem demonstrate that mastery of proportional reasoning requires integrating all the strands of proficiency. They all solved the problem, but each child used a different technique, some more sophisticated than others. They did not just randomly perform operations on the numbers, as Damon started to do. They all understood that the relationship between the balloons and the dollars must remain the same, as Belinda's circles and column of \$2s illustrate.

Being fluent with various computational procedures such as counting, multiplying, and dividing helped each student attack the problem. Each child also was able to reason about the situation and to explain to the others what he or she was doing. They all expected to be able to make sense of the problem and persisted until they reached a solution they were sure of, even though Damon began with two different answers and Marti with a "wacky number."

This example illustrates how students can use their own sense-making skills to get started in a complex domain such as this. As they gain more experience with proportional situations, they can continue to develop and learn more efficient methods without losing contact with the other strands of mathematical proficiency.

Developing Proficiency Throughout the Elementary and Middle School Years

Mathematical proficiency cannot be characterized as simply present or absent. Every important mathematical idea can be understood at many levels and in many ways. Obviously, a first grader's understanding of addition is not the same as that of a mathematician or even an average adult. But a first grader can still be proficient with single-digit addition, as long as his or her thinking in that realm incorporates all five strands of proficiency.

Proficiency in mathematics develops over time. Thus, each year they are in school, students ought to become increasingly proficient with both old and new content. For example, third graders should be more proficient with the addition of whole numbers than they were in first grade. But in every grade, students ought to be able to demonstrate mathematical proficiency in some form.

Developing Proficiency in All Students

Historically, school mathematics policy in the United States was based on the assumption that only a select group of learners should be expected to become proficient in mathematics. That assumption is no longer tenable. Young people who are unable to think mathematically are denied many of the best opportunities that society offers, and society is denied their potential contributions.

Many adults assume that differences in mathematics performance reflect differences in innate ability, rather than differences in individual effort or opportunities to learn. These expectations profoundly underestimate what children can do. The basic principles, concepts, and skills of mathematics are within reach of all children. When parents and teachers alike believe that hard work pays off, and when mathematics is taught and learned by using all the strands of proficiency, mathematics performance improves for all students.

Careful research has demonstrated that mathematical proficiency is an obtainable goal. In a handful of schools scattered across the country, high percentages of students from all backgrounds have achieved high levels of performance in mathematics. Special interventions in some low-performing schools have produced substantial progress. More is now known about how children learn mathematics and the kinds of teaching that support progress.

Research evidence demonstrates that all but a very small number of students can learn to read proficiently. They may learn at different rates and may require different amounts and types of instructional support to learn to read well, but all can become proficient in reading.[9] The same is true of learning and doing mathematics.

What is wrong with the old ways of teaching math?

Teaching focused on one strand at a time—such as mastering computational procedures followed by problem solving—has not helped most students to achieve math proficiency. Results of major national studies dating back decades suggest that students have never been particularly successful in developing computational skills beyond whole numbers, and they have been very unsuccessful in applying the skills they have learned.[10] They also haven't demonstrated much understanding of the math concepts used in either computation or problem solving.

How can teachers develop all the strands of math proficiency when they already have so much to teach?

By teaching math in an integrated fashion, teachers will actually save time in the long run. They will eliminate the need to go over the same content time and again because students did not learn it well in the first place. They will not spend so much time on a single strand, deferring the other strands until students "are ready." Rather, the five strands will support one another, which will make learning more effective and enduring.

Success in Classrooms of Disadvantaged Students

The evidence from research suggests that students can achieve proficiency if mathematics is taught in a coherent, integrated way. For example, a large-scale study of 150 first-grade to sixth-grade classrooms serving low-income families demonstrated the advantages of teaching for mathematical proficiency. One set of classrooms used a conventional computation-oriented curriculum. Another set stressed conceptual understanding and expanded the range of mathematical topics included in the curriculum beyond arithmetic.

In the latter classrooms, teachers used multiple representations of mathematical ideas to support understanding, focused on nonroutine problems to strengthen application of concepts, emphasized multiple solutions to problems to develop computing fluency, and held classroom discussions requiring logical reasoning that explored alternative solutions or meanings of mathematical procedures or results.

Students in the latter classrooms performed substantially better than those in the conventional classrooms. At the end of the two-year study, these students not only had a greater grasp of advanced skills but also had better computational skills. Similar results were found for reading and writing.

A commonly held myth in education is that students in high-poverty classrooms should not engage in academically challenging work until they have mastered the basic skills. This study dispels that myth. It shows that teaching that is organized around all the strands of mathematical proficiency is especially appropriate and effective with disadvantaged students.[11]

Investigations

How Does School Mathematics Need to Change for All Students to Become Mathematically Proficient?

To achieve the goal of mathematical proficiency for all, many components of U.S. school mathematics must be changed. In particular, instruction, instructional materials, assessments, teacher education and professional development, and the broader educational system must work together to ensure that all students become engaged with mathematics throughout their elementary and middle school years. The following sections address each of these five areas of needed change.

Instruction Needs to Support the Development of Mathematical Proficiency for All

Whether students will become proficient in mathematics depends in large part on the instruction they receive. Teaching that builds proficiency can take many forms; although there is no best way to teach, not all ways of teaching are equally effective. The key question to ask about any instance of instruction is: Does it provide opportunities for students to develop all five strands of mathematical proficiency?[12]

Teaching for proficiency requires thoughtful planning, careful execution, and continual improvement of instruction. Lessons need to be designed with specific mathematical learning goals in mind. Teachers must ask: How will this lesson help students develop and integrate the strands of proficiency? How will students' learning in this lesson build on past lessons and set the stage for later lessons? What knowledge do students bring with them to this lesson, and how are they likely to respond to the mathematical tasks it contains? What materials and activities can help students achieve the goals for the lesson?

Proficiency is much more likely to develop when a mathematics classroom is a community of learners rather than a collection of isolated individuals. In such a classroom, students are encouraged to generate and share solution methods, mistakes are valued as opportunities for everyone to learn, and correctness is determined by the logic and structure of the problem, rather than by the teacher. Questioning and discussion that elicit students' thinking and solution strategies and build on those strategies lead to greater clarity and precision. A significant amount of class time is spent developing mathematical ideas, not just practicing skills.[13]

In addition to working as members of the classroom community, students also need to become independent learners, both inside and outside the classroom. Students should have opportunities to work independently of the teacher, individually and in pairs or groups. When homework is assigned for the purpose of developing skills, students should be sufficiently familiar with the skills so that they do not practice incorrect procedures. Only by becoming independent learners can students come to see mathematics as doable and useful.

One of the strongest findings from research is that time and opportunity to learn are essential for successful learning. For all students to develop mathematical proficiency, schools should devote a substantial and regular amount of time to mathematics instruction. As an overall guideline, an hour each school day should be devoted to mathematics instruction from kindergarten through eighth grade. This time should be apportioned so that all the strands of mathematical proficiency receive adequate attention.

Does working in small groups help students to develop math proficiency?

It depends. Students in groups—sometimes called cooperative groups—of three, four, or five can work on a math task together and thereby increase their proficiency. But if the task does not allow each student to contribute, and if students are not sure what they are supposed to do, precious learning time is wasted. When used appropriately, small groups can both increase achievement and promote positive social interactions among students.[14] But for groups to be effective, tasks must be well chosen and students must be taught how to work in this mode.

Don't students have to be grouped by ability to develop math proficiency?

"Ability grouping" in elementary and middle school, in which students are separated into classes based on test scores or math grades, is really grouping by achievement, and it tends to be self-perpetuating. Students placed in lower groups receive fewer opportunities to develop all the strands of math proficiency. Their classes typically have a less demanding curriculum, less capable teachers, and few or no strong peer models. As a result, achievement gaps grow rather than diminish, and socioeconomic, racial, and ethnic disparities widen.[15]

These observations suggest that the wiser course in elementary and middle school grades is not to group students into classes by ability or achievement. Accelerated classes are not necessary to help high-achieving students learn more; this can be accomplished within mixed groups. Some countries with impressive math achievement scores do not separate high achievers from low achievers. Effective teaching methods can help all students in mixed-ability classes to develop proficiency, and teachers can be supported to acquire and use these methods.

Instructional Materials Need to Integrate the Strands of Mathematical Proficiency

Textbooks and other instructional materials in the United States need to support the learning of all five strands of mathematical proficiency. They should develop the core content of mathematics in a focused way and with continuity within and across grades. More time should be spent developing fewer topics in each grade, as is done in many countries where mathematics achievement is strong.[16] Textbooks should move on to new, more advanced topics and should develop those in depth rather than repeating many topics every year.

Instructional materials need to have teacher notes that support teachers' understanding of mathematical concepts, student thinking and student errors, and effective pedagogical supports and techniques. Instructional materials should incorporate activities and strategies that assist teachers in helping all students become proficient in mathematics, including students low in socioeconomic status, English-language learners, special education students, and students with special interests or talents in mathematics.

Assessments Need to Contribute to the Goal of Mathematical Proficiency

In recent years, many states and districts have mandated a variety of assessments to measure the mathematics performance of students. Some of these assessments have serious consequences for students, teachers, and schools, such as determining whether a student will graduate or whether a school will avoid state sanctions. In some cases, the assessment aims at what students have mastered, and all students should be able to demonstrate mastery. In many other cases, however, the assessment ranks students, schools, or districts; this means that half of those being assessed are necessarily below par. Such assessments typically do not provide information that can be used to improve instruction.

The goal of mathematical proficiency for all requires as one of its first tasks a rethinking of what assessments are measuring. Large-scale comparisons are seldom aligned with the curriculum and often focus on only one or two aspects of

Why are students playing with blocks, sticks, and beans in math classes?

Reflecting on the use of physical objects—such as blocks, sticks, and beans—can help students to develop understanding by linking their informal knowledge and experiences to school math.[17] However, much depends on how these objects are used. Physical materials should not be used simply as tools to calculate answers. Students need to be able to move from using physical objects to finding solutions numerically. Teachers must provide opportunities for students to make explicit connections between activities with the objects and the math concepts and procedures that the objects are intended to help teach. The math is in the connections, not the objects.

Should all students study algebra?

Yes. Algebra is the gateway to higher math. Proficiency in algebra helps students solidify their proficiency in numbers and integrate their knowledge of math. Algebra provides the concepts and language to move from individual numerical calculations to general relationships. The study of algebra, however, need not begin with a formal course in the subject. The elementary and middle school curriculum can support the development of algebraic ways of thinking and thereby avoid the difficulties many students now experience in making the transition from arithmetic to algebra. The basic ideas of algebra can be learned by the end of middle school if they are taught in ways that draw on and develop all strands of math proficiency.

performance.[18] Preparing for and taking tests that do not measure the five strands of proficiency consume time that could be devoted to teaching and learning mathematics.

All assessments need to support the development of mathematical proficiency. They need to measure the five strands of proficiency and their integration. By doing so, they will provide opportunities for students to become proficient rather than taking time away from this goal. Teachers' informal assessments of student progress provide valuable information as they adjust their instruction to help their students become proficient. More formal assessments also can help to track students' progress and identify areas in which they need help.

As large-scale formal assessments become increasingly popular, the goal of supporting the development of students' mathematical proficiency could be furthered if a government agency were to fund an independent group to analyze these assessment programs for the extent to which they promote mathematical proficiency. This group could recommend how such programs might be modified to promote the goal of proficiency.

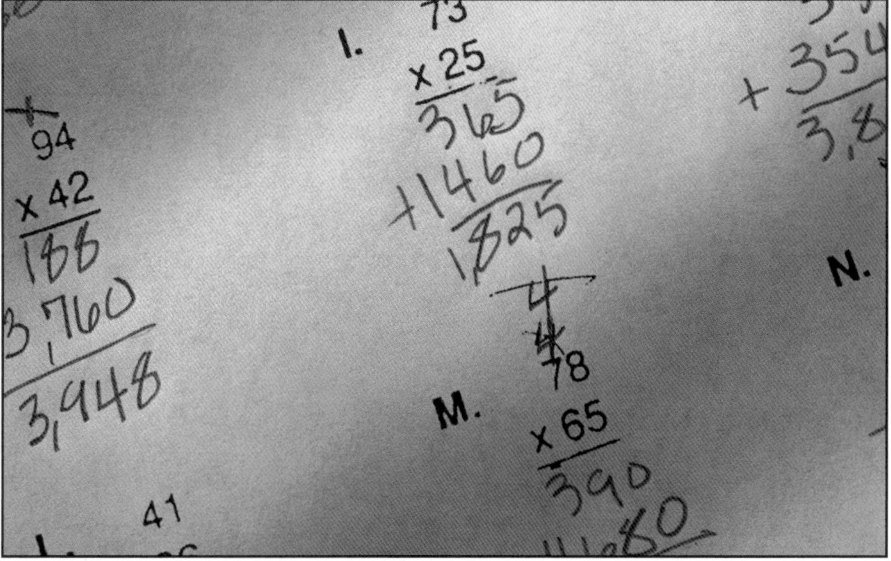

Teachers Need Support That Will Enable Them to Teach All Students to Be Mathematically Proficient

Like any complex task, effective mathematics teaching must be learned. Teachers need a special kind of knowledge. To teach mathematics well, they must themselves be proficient in mathematics, at a much deeper level than their students. They also must understand how students develop mathematical proficiency, and they must have a repertoire of teaching practices that can promote proficiency. Unfortunately, very few teachers have the specialized knowledge needed to teach mathematics in the ways envisioned in this report.[19] The view of mathematical proficiency presented here requires that teachers act in new ways and have knowledge and understanding they once were not expected to have.

Like learning in any profession, learning to teach for mathematical proficiency is a career-long challenge. Acquiring this knowledge and learning how to use it effectively in the classroom will take not only time but resources. Professional development must become a continuing part of the teacher's workweek rather than taking the form of an occasional workshop.[20] Teachers need extensive opportunities to learn, to observe models of effective practice, and to have access to expertise in mathematics teaching. It is not reasonable in the short term to expect all teachers to acquire the knowledge they need to teach for mathematical proficiency. To further promote effective teaching and learning, mathematics specialists—teachers who have special training and interest in mathematics—should be available in every elementary school.

The undergraduate years of teacher training must provide significant and continuing opportunities, linked closely to classroom practice, for prospective teachers to develop the knowledge needed to teach for mathematical proficiency. Prospective teachers must study students' thinking and relate that thinking to the kinds of mathematical knowledge that students bring with them to school. People intending to be teachers must continue developing their own mathematical proficiency and learn how to use that proficiency to guide discussions, modify problems, and make decisions about what to pursue in class. They cannot wait until they enter the profession to learn to teach effectively.

Does improving students' math proficiency require new types of tests?

Yes. New tests may be needed, and old tests may need to be changed. Most current math tests, whether standardized achievement tests or classroom quizzes, address only a fraction of math proficiency—usually just the computing strand and simple parts of the understanding and applying strands. Teachers need tests and other assessment procedures that let them gauge how far students have come along in all five proficiency strands. Furthermore, instead of taking time away from learning, these instruments should allow students simultaneously to build and exhibit their proficiency.

Efforts to Achieve Mathematical Proficiency Must Be Coordinated, Comprehensive, and Informed by Scientific Evidence

Many people have worked very hard in recent years to change the ways in which mathematics is taught and learned. However, the problem requires greater and different efforts than those made so far. Complex systems like school mathematics are what social scientists call overdetermined. A large number of pressures exert forces on these systems, making them remarkably stable and resistant to change. Altering such a system requires the coordinated efforts of everyone involved.

Mathematical proficiency for all is an ambitious objective. In fact, in no country—not even those that have performed better than the United States on international comparisons of mathematics achievement—do all students display mathematical proficiency as defined in this book. Reaching this goal will require fundamental changes in many areas of school mathematics.

The only way to achieve long-term improvement is through a coherent and systematic approach. This will require that all aspects of the system be reformed simultaneously. We therefore conclude with a list of actions that the individuals and groups to whom this book is addressed must take to achieve the goal of mathematical proficiency for all. By pursuing these actions in a coordinated and resolute fashion, those people involved in mathematics education in the United States can drive changes that will have substantial and lasting benefits for all students and for the nation as a whole.

What Can Parents and Caregivers Do?

Before Children Enter School

Just as parents can help their children be ready to learn to read, they can give children a good start in learning math by helping them develop proficiency with informal math concepts and skills.

- Play games such as dominoes and board games.
- Find natural opportunities to count, to sort objects, to match collections of objects, to identify shapes (while reading bedtime stories, going up stairs, setting the table, etc.).
- Count a collection of objects and use number words to identify very small collections.
- Talk with your child about simple math problems and ideas. (How many spoons do we need to set the table? Give me the cup with the two flowers on it. Find the other circle on this page. Sort the blocks by shape.)

After Children Enter School

- Have high expectations. Children's math achievement is shaped—and limited—by what is expected of them.

- Expect some confusion to be part of the learning process but emphasize that effort, not ability, is what counts. Math is understandable and can be figured out.

- Avoid conveying negative attitudes toward math. Never tell children to not worry about a certain kind of math because it will never be used.

- Ask your child what he or she did in math class today. Ask him or her to give details and to explain.

- Expect your child's homework to include more than simple computation worksheets.

- Give your child meaningful problems that use numbers or shapes while you are going about everyday life. Ask the child to explain what he or she did.

- Be an advocate for the theme of math proficiency in textbooks, assessments, and instruction.

- Advocate allocating and using a regular time each school day for instruction to develop math proficiency.

- Support professional development activities for teachers and administrators.

What Can Teachers Do?

- Be committed to the idea that all children can become proficient in math.
- Develop and deepen your understanding of math, of student thinking, and of techniques that promote math proficiency.
- Emphasize to policy makers, administrators, parents, and students the need for and the achievability of math proficiency.
- Use an instructional program and materials that, based on the best available scientific evidence, support the development of math proficiency.
- Teach mathematics for a sufficient amount of time (e.g., an hour a day).
- Attend professional development activities that integrate math, student thinking, and instructional techniques.
- Advocate for ongoing, sustained, coherent professional development activities that support teaching for math proficiency.
- Organize and participate in study groups at your school that focus on teaching practice.
- Engage in conversations with colleagues about developing proficiency and about students and their math proficiency.
- Become a mentor to a colleague learning to teach for math proficiency.

What Can Administrators Do?

- Embrace the overarching goal of math proficiency for all.
- Promote the idea to teachers and parents that math proficiency for all is both desirable and achievable.
- Become an instructional leader in your school.
- Spend time in math classrooms observing teachers and coaching teachers on teaching for proficiency.
- Provide for a math curriculum aligned with the goal of math proficiency and expect teachers to design their instructional program accordingly.
- Hire one or more math specialists for each elementary school.
- Ensure that sufficient time is allocated for learning math.
- Provide time and resources for ongoing district-wide and school-based professional development focused on math.
- Make available teacher stipends, released time, and other support for substantial and sustained professional development.
- Focus on coherent, multi-year programs.
- Attend staff development activities for administrators to become familiar with math proficiency and with how proficiency is attained.

What Can Policy Makers Do?

- Embrace the overarching goal of math proficiency for all.
- Stress to interested stakeholders the need to accomplish this goal.
- Support the allocation of scarce education resources to bring about needed critical changes.

  —Realign curricula to promote math proficiency.

  —Fund independent groups to assess alignment of textbooks and testing to achieve math proficiency.

  —Encourage the expenditure of time and resources for necessary and sustained teacher professional development.

  —Support the placement of one or more math specialists in each elementary school.
- Maintain consistency with the above by supporting the concept that, whenever possible, education decisions should be based on evidence.
- Take full advantage of the current national focus on and interest in improving education.

NOTES

1. For more details see Chapter 2 "The State of School Mathematics in the United States" (pp. 31-70) in: National Research Council. (2001). *Adding it up: Helping children learn mathematics.* Mathematics Learning Study Committee, J. Kilpatrick, J. Swafford, B. Findell, Editors. Center for Education, Division of Behavioral and Social Sciences and Education. Washington, DC: National Academy Press.

2. For information on the Third International Mathematics and Science Study benchmarking studies, visit http://www.nces.ed.gov/timss/timss95/benchmark.asp [September 25, 2001].

See also Reese, C.M., Miller, K.E., Mazzeo, J., & Dossey, J.A. (1997). *NAEP 1996 mathematics report card for the nation and the states* (NCES 97-488). Washington, DC: National Center for Education Statistics. Available: http://nces.ed.gov/spider/webspider/97488.shtml [September 25, 2001].

See also Campbell, J.R., Voelkl, K.E., & Donahue, P.L. (2000). *NAEP 1996 trends in academic progress* (NCES 97-985r). Washington, DC: National Center for Education Statistics. Available: http://nces.ed.gov/spider/webspider/97985r.shtml [September 25, 2001].

3. In the full report, the five strands are labeled somewhat differently: conceptual understanding, procedural fluency, strategic competence, adaptive reasoning, and productive disposition. Although the labels have been simplified in this report, their descriptions reflect those in the full report.

4. For a fuller discussion of this research, see the section on Calculators (pp. 354-356) in Chapter 9 "Teaching for Mathematical Proficiency" in *Adding It Up.*

5. See the section on Subtraction Algorithms (pp. 204-206) in Chapter 6 "Developing Proficiency with Whole Numbers" in *Adding It Up.*

6. For a review of the research and a more detailed discussion of how children learn basic number combinations, see Chapter 6 "Developing Proficiency with Whole Numbers" (pp. 181-229) in *Adding It Up.*

7. Ben-Chaim, D., Fey, J.T., Fitzgerald, W.M., Benedetto, C., & Miller, J. (1998). Proportional reasoning among 7th grade students with different curricular experiences. *Educational Studies in Mathematics, 36,* 247-273.

8. Langrall, C.W., & Swafford, J.O. (2000). Three balloons for two dollars: Developing proportional reasoning. *Mathematics Teaching in the Middle School, 6,* 254-261.

9. National Research Council. (1998). *Preventing reading difficulties in young children.* Committee on the Prevention of Reading Difficulties in Young Children, C.E. Snow, M.S. Burns, and P. Griffin, Editors. Commission on Behavioral and Social Sciences and Education. Washington, DC: National Academy Press. Available: http://books.nap.edu/catalog/6023.html

See also Silver, E.A., & Kenney, P.A. (2000). *Results from the seventh mathematics assessment of the National Assessment of Educational Progress.* Reston, VA: National Council of Teachers of Mathematics.

See also Thorndike, E.L. (1922). *The psychology of arithmetic.* New York: Macmillan.

10. Campbell, J.R., Voelkl, K.E., & Donahue, P.L. (2000). *NAEP 1996 trends in academic progress* (NCES 97-985r). Washington, DC: National Center for Education Statistics. Available: http://nces.ed.gov/spider/webspider/97985r.shtml [September 25, 2001].

11. Knapp, M.S., Shields, P.M., & Turnbull, B.J. (1995, June). Academic challenge in high-poverty classrooms. *Phi Delta Kappan, 76,* 770-776.

12. See pages 315-333 of Chapter 9 "Teaching for Mathematical Proficiency" in *Adding It Up* for four classroom vignettes illustrating different images of mathematics instruction.

13. See the discussion of Communities of Learners (pp. 344-345) in Chapter 9 "Teaching for Mathematical Proficiency" in *Adding It Up.*

14. For a fuller discussion of the research, see the section on Cooperative Groups (pp. 348-349) in Chapter 9 "Teaching for Mathematical Proficiency" in *Adding It Up.*

15. For a fuller discussion of the research, see the section on Grouping (pp. 346-348) in Chapter 9 "Teaching for Mathematical Proficiency" in *Adding It Up.*

16. See the section on Instructional Programs and Materials (pp. 36-39) in Chapter 2 "The State of School Mathematics in the United States" in *Adding It Up.*

17. See the section on Manipulatives (pp. 353-354) in Chapter 9 "Teaching for Mathematical Proficiency" in *Adding It Up.*

18. See the section on Assessments (pp. 39-44) in Chapter 2 "The State of School Mathematics in the United States" in *Adding It Up.*

19. See the section on Knowledge of Mathematics (pp. 372-378) in Chapter 10 "Developing Proficiency in Teaching Mathematics" in *Adding It Up.*

20. See the section on Programs to Develop Proficient Teaching (pp. 385-397) in Chapter 10 "Developing Proficiency in Teaching Mathematics" in *Adding It Up* for a description of four different approaches to professional development and teacher education.

CREDITS

Cover: *left and center,* ©PhotoDisc; *right,* Richard B. Lacampagne

Page i: ©PhotoDisc

Page 2: *left,* Richard B. Lacampagne; *top right,* Paul Baker; *bottom,* Paul Baker

Page 4: Richard B. Lacampagne

Page 17: Richard B. Lacampagne

Page 19: Richard B. Lacampagne

Page 23: Paul Baker

Page 24: *left,* Paul Baker; *top and right,* ©PhotoDisc

Page 26: Paul Baker

Page 28: Richard B. Lacampagne

Page 30: ©PhotoDisc

Page 34: *left,* ©PhotoDisc; *top*, Paul Baker; *right,* ©PhotoDisc

Helping Children Learn Mathematics

Results from national and international assessments indicate that school children in the United States are not learning mathematics well enough. Many students cannot correctly apply computational algorithms to solve problems. Their understanding and use of decimals and fractions are especially weak. Indeed, helping all children succeed in mathematics is an imperative national goal.

Based on the National Research Councilís 2001 release, *Adding It Up*, this concise and informative booklet explains the five key strands of mathematical proficiency and discusses the major changes that need to be made in mathematics instruction, instructional materials, assessments, teacher education, and the broader educational system.

What does it mean to be successful in mathematics? How can all students become mathematically proficient? Addressing these questions and more, **Helping Children Learn Mathematics** explains how school mathematics needs to change to prepare students for life in the 21st century.

Also of interest...

Adding It Up: Helping Children Learn Mathematics

The full report on which *Helping Children Learn Mathematics* is based. This book identifies the interdependent components of mathematical proficiency and makes sweeping recommendations for helping students develop proficiency.

ISBN 0-309-06995-5, 480 pages, 7 x 10, cloth w/ jacket (2001)

Investigating the Influence of Standards

This book provides a framework to guide the design, conduct, and interpretation of research regarding the influences of nationally promulgated education standards.

ISBN 0-309-07276-X, 152 pages, 7 x 10, paperback (2001)

Scientific Research in Education

Describes the similarities and differences between scientific inquiry in education and scientific inquiry in other fields and disciplines, providing numerous examples to illustrate these ideas.

ISBN 0-309-08291-9, 204 pages, 6 x 9, paperback (2002)

Use the form on the reverse of this card to order your copies today.

Helping Children Learn Mathematics

Results from national and international assessments indicate that school children in the United States are not learning mathematics well enough. Many students cannot correctly apply computational algorithms to solve problems. Their understanding and use of decimals and fractions are especially weak. Indeed, helping all children succeed in mathematics is an imperative national goal.

Based on the National Research Councilís 2001 release, *Adding It Up*, this concise and informative booklet explains the five key strands of mathematical proficiency and discusses the major changes that need to be made in mathematics instruction, instructional materials, assessments, teacher education, and the broader educational system.

What does it mean to be successful in mathematics? How can all students become mathematically proficient? Addressing these questions and more, **Helping Children Learn Mathematics** explains how school mathematics needs to change to prepare students for life in the 21st century.

Also of interest...

Adding It Up: Helping Children Learn Mathematics

The full report on which *Helping Children Learn Mathematics* is based. This book identifies the interdependent components of mathematical proficiency and makes sweeping recommendations for helping students develop proficiency.

ISBN 0-309-06995-5, 480 pages, 7 x 10, cloth w/ jacket (2001)

Investigating the Influence of Standards

This book provides a framework to guide the design, conduct, and interpretation of research regarding the influences of nationally promulgated education standards.

ISBN 0-309-07276-X, 152 pages, 7 x 10, paperback (2001)

Scientific Research in Education

Describes the similarities and differences between scientific inquiry in education and scientific inquiry in other fields and disciplines, providing numerous examples to illustrate these ideas.

ISBN 0-309-08291-9, 204 pages, 6 x 9, paperback (2002)

Use the form on the reverse of this card to order your copies today.

ORDER CARD
(Customers in North America Only)

Helping Children Learn Mathematics

Use this card to order additional copies of **Helping Children Learn Mathematics** and the book described on the reverse. All orders must be prepaid. Please add $4.50 for shipping and handling for the first copy ordered and $0.95 for each additional copy. If you live in CA, DC, FL, MA, MD, MO, TX, or Canada, add applicable sales tax or GST. Prices apply only in the United States, Canada, and Mexico and are subject to change without notice.

___ I am enclosing a U.S. check or money order.

___ Please charge my VISA/MasterCard/American Express account.

Number: ______________________

Expiration date: ______________________

Signature: ______________________

PLEASE SEND ME:

Qty.	ISBN	Title	Price
____	8431-8	Helping Children Learn Mathematics	$10.00
____	6995-5	Adding It Up	$29.95
____	7276-X	Investigating the Influence of Standards	$24.95
____	8291-9	Scientific Research in Education	$25.00

Please print.

Name ______________________

Address ______________________

City ______________________ State _____ ZIP __________

8431

FOUR EASY WAYS TO ORDER

- **Electronically:** Order from our secure website at: **www.nap.edu**
- **By phone:** Call toll-free 1-800-624-6242 or (202) 334-3313 or call your favorite bookstore.
- **By fax:** Copy the order card and fax to (202) 334-2451.
- **By mail:** Return this card with your payment to NATIONAL ACADEMY PRESS, 2101 Constitution Avenue, NW, Lockbox 285, Washington, DC 20055.

Quantity Discounts: 2-9copies, $8.50; 10-49 copies, $6.00; 50-00 copies, $4.50; 100-499 copies, $3.00. For orders of 500+ please contact us for a price quote. To be eligible for a discount, all copies must be shipped and billed to one address.

All international customers please contact National Academy Press for export prices and ordering information.

ORDER CARD
(Customers in North America Only)

Helping Children Learn Mathematics

Use this card to order additional copies of **Helping Children Learn Mathematics** and the book described on the reverse. All orders must be prepaid. Please add $4.50 for shipping and handling for the first copy ordered and $0.95 for each additional copy. If you live in CA, DC, FL, MA, MD, MO, TX, or Canada, add applicable sales tax or GST. Prices apply only in the United States, Canada, and Mexico and are subject to change without notice.

___ I am enclosing a U.S. check or money order.

___ Please charge my VISA/MasterCard/American Express account.

Number: ______________________

Expiration date: ______________________

Signature: ______________________

PLEASE SEND ME:

Qty.	ISBN	Title	Price
____	8431-8	Helping Children Learn Mathematics	$10.00
____	6995-5	Adding It Up	$29.95
____	7276-X	Investigating the Influence of Standards	$24.95
____	8291-9	Scientific Research in Education	$25.00

Please print.

Name ______________________

Address ______________________

City ______________________ State _____ ZIP __________

8431

FOUR EASY WAYS TO ORDER

- **Electronically:** Order from our secure website at: **www.nap.edu**
- **By phone:** Call toll-free 1-800-624-6242 or (202) 334-3313 or call your favorite bookstore.
- **By fax:** Copy the order card and fax to (202) 334-2451.
- **By mail:** Return this card with your payment to NATIONAL ACADEMY PRESS, 2101 Constitution Avenue, NW, Lockbox 285, Washington, DC 20055.

Quantity Discounts: 2-9copies, $8.50; 10-49 copies, $6.00; 50-00 copies, $4.50; 100-499 copies, $3.00. For orders of 500+ please contact us for a price quote. To be eligible for a discount, all copies must be shipped and billed to one address.

All international customers please contact National Academy Press for export prices and ordering information.